ARE YOU A WASP?
Take this quick quiz and find out!

DO YOU . . .
Talk like William F. Buckley?
Look like John Houseman?
Have the politics of Ronald Reagan?
The sure-footedness of Gerald Ford?

If you checked any of these then you're a bona-fide WASP-in-training! If you didn't check any, then breathe a sigh of relief! At least you're not *that* bad off! So kick back, open the book, and get ready to laugh yourself silly, or WASPy, whichever comes first!

BOOKS by LARRY WILDE

The Official All America Joke Book
The *Ultimate* Lawyers Joke Book
The *Ultimate* Jewish Joke Book
More The Official Doctors Joke Book
The Official Executives Joke Book
The Official Sports Maniacs Joke Book
The *Absolutely Last* Official Sex Maniacs Joke Book
The Official Book of John Jokes
The Official Politicians Joke Book
The Official Rednecks Joke Book
The *Last* Official Smart Kids Joke Book
The *Absolutely Last* Official Polish Joke Book
The *Last* Official Irish Joke Book
The *Last* Official Sex Maniacs Joke Book
The Larry Wilde Book of Limericks
The Official Lawyers Joke Book
The Official Doctors Joke Book
More The Official Sex Maniacs Joke Book
The *Last* Official Jewish Joke Book

   also

The Official Bedroom/Bathroom Joke Book
More The Official Smart Kids/Dumb Parents Joke Book
The Official Book of Sick Jokes
More The Official Jewish/Irish Joke Book
The *Last* Official Italian Joke Book
The Official Cat Lovers/Dog Lovers Joke Book
The Official Dirty Joke Book
The *Last* Official Polish Joke Book
The Official Golfers Joke Book
The Official Smart Kids/Dumb Parents Joke Book
The Official Religious/Not So Religious Joke Book
More The Official Polish/Italian Joke Book
The Official Black Folks/White Folks Joke Book
The Official Virgins/Sex Maniacs Joke Book
The Official Jewish/Irish Joke Book
The Official Polish/Italian Joke Book

   and in hardcover

THE COMPLETE BOOK OF ETHNIC HUMOR
HOW THE GREAT COMEDY WRITERS CREATE
   LAUGHTER
THE GREAT COMEDIANS TALK ABOUT COMEDY

THE OFFICIAL W.A.S.P. JOKE BOOK

LARRY WILDE

BANTAM BOOKS

TORONTO · NEW YORK · LONDON · SYDNEY · AUCKLAND

THE OFFICIAL WASP JOKE BOOK

A Bantam Book / May 1988

Illustrated by Ron Wing.

ISBN 0-553-27069-9

Published simultaneously in the United States and Canada

Bantam Books are published by Bantam Books, a division
of Bantam Doubleday Dell Publishing Group, Inc. Its trade-
mark, consisting of the words ''Bantam Books'' and the por-
trayal of a rooster, is Registered in U.S. Patent and Trademark
Office and in other countries. Marca Registrada, Bantam
Books, 666 Fifth Avenue, New York, New York 10103.

PRINTED IN THE UNITED STATES OF AMERICA

O   0 9 8 7 6 5 4 3 2 1

For my friend
Fred Feuille

CONTENTS

Introduction

What in the world is a WASP?

You mean you don't know?

WASPs are the most privileged, influential, and wealthiest minority in U.S. society. What's more, they are probably the only minority that has never suffered prejudice because of race or religion.

Officially, W.A.S.P. stands for *White Anglo Saxon Protestant*. Depending on who you talk to, WASP can also mean *We Are Selfish & Pompous*. Some pundits even say the letters indicate *We Are Selfish Pricks.*

There are many ways in which to identify members of other minorities superficially. It is fairly easy to recognize Black, Chinese, Italian, Jewish, Irish, and Polish people by their color, names, and certain distinguishable and behavioral characteristics.

The same holds true for WASPs. Here's what *The American Heritage Dictionary* says:

> *WASP—a white U.S. citizen of nonspecific or religious identity.*

But some definitions can best be delivered through humor:

> *How many WASPs does it take to screw in a light bulb?*
> *Two. One to call the electrician, the other to make the martinis.*

Here's the stand-up comedians' view:

> *A WASP is a person who thinks Taco Bell is a Mexican phone company.*

> *A WASP is a white-collar redneck.*

> *A WASP is a person who thinks a unicorn is a horse with an erection in the wrong place.*

You still don't know what a WASP is?

Perhaps the best way to come up with an answer to the question is to examine the idiosyncracies of this indestructible clan. For example, Eating habits:

> *How many courses in a WASP dinner?*
> *Seven. Six martinis and a cheese-and-cracker.*

> *What's a seven-course meal to a Georgetown preppie?*
> *A Big Mac and a six-pack.*

Here's an observation by the Washington wit, Mark Russell:

> *Why didn't the WASP finish eating his corned beef sandwich at the Woodmont Country Club?*
> *Because the chef ran out of raisin bread.*

How about his married life?

> *Willoughby and Cavendish were sitting in the country club locker room after a round of golf. "Lets get our wives together tonight and have a big, fun evening," said Willoughby.*
> *"Okay," retorted Cavendish. "But where shall we leave them?"*

Daffie and Mylow were driving home from a Sunday brunch at a friend's house. Finally, Daffie broke the long silence and asked, "Why did you tell Wainwright you married me because I'm such a wonderful cook? I can't boil a potato."

"But I had to give some excuse," snapped her husband.

Then there's the recognition factor:

What do you get when you cross a WASP with an ape?

A hairy Chairman of the Board.

How do you recognize a WASP at a nudist colony?

He's the one with The Wall Street Journal *on his lap.*

What about background?

"My family can trace its lineage back to Leif Ericsson," stated Townely.

"Really?" questioned Driscoll. "Next thing you'll tell me is that your family sailed with Noah on the Ark."

"Nonsense," declared Townely. "My family has always had their own boats."

But wait, do they have a sense of humor?

> *Rizzutti and Giordano were lunching at the Palmer House in Chicago. "What makes you think WASPs even have a sense of humor?" asked Rizzutti.*
>
> *"Don't be silly! Of course WASPs know humor!" retorted Giordano. "A WASP laughs at a joke three times. Once when he hears it, once when it's explained to him, and once when he understands it."*

You say you still don't know what a WASP is?

You say you can't believe that a group like this actually exists?

You say a species of human beings couldn't possibly be that ridiculous or ludicrous or foolishly funny?

Tell you what I'm gonna do! I'm gonna let you judge for yourself. In the following pages you will find the WASP in his natural habitat. From Chatham, Massachusetts, to Bellevue, Washington. From the Nantucket Yacht Club to the St. Francis in San Francisco—they're all here!

The Preppies and Mummys and Daddys and Nannys and all the folks in patchwork pants, embroidered corduroys, Shetland sweaters, button-down shirts, and seersucker suits. You are holding in your hands the consummate comic bible of whimsical WASP-hood. Have fun!

LARRY WILDE

The Daddys

"Say, Bradford, are you awake? There's a burglar downstairs!"
"No, I'm asleep!"

*   *   *

A small Massachusetts town decided to buy a new fire truck. When the city council met, they got into a discussion about what to do with the old one.

"I think," said Merriweather, father of four, "that we should keep the old fire truck and use it for false alarms."

*   *   *

Bentley entered the bedroom, undressed quickly, and crawled into bed. He leaned over and kissed his wife on the cheek. Then he waited a moment and gave her a resounding wallop on the behind.

"What's that for?" she shrieked, jumping up in bed.

"For not opening your eyes to see who it was!"

*   *   *

The Buffums were sitting in the living room watching television.

"Say," said the wife, "do you think Cybill Shepherd is her real name?"

Buffum thought for a minute and then replied, "Do I think whose real name is Cybill Shepherd?"

*   *   *

OVERHEARD AT COUNTRY CLUB

Mummy: You shouldn't be swimming on a full stomach.
Daddy: Okay, I'll swim on my back.

*   *   *

At the country club, Caldwell could talk on any subject you chose, whether he knew anything about the topic or not. Mostly he didn't. Finally, his neighbor, Ratchford, could stand no more.

"Do you realize," said Ratchford, "that you and I know all there is to be known?"

"Do you think so, old man?" said Caldwell. "How do you figure that?"

"Easy," said Ratchford, "you know everything except that you are a damn idiot. And I know that."

Mead: I hate to say it, *dah*ling, but this
      toast is really tough.
Lisa: You're eating the paper plate, *deah*!

* * *

Shingles were coming loose on Pennock's
Bernardsville house, and he complained of
the leaks to Grange, his neighbor.

"Why don't you mend the roof?" asked
Grange.

"I can't today, it's pouring rain."

"Well, why don't you have the roof
mended in dry weather?"

"It doesn't leak then," said Pennock.

* * *

Cockwell, following taillights in a dense
fog, crashed into the car ahead of him when
it stopped suddenly. "Why didn't you let
me know you were going to stop?" Cockwell
shouted.

"Why should I?" came a voice out of
the fog. "I'm in my own garage!"

* * *

Tiffany was visiting her bandaged husband in a hospital. On the way out, she said
to the nurse, "My husband always says,
'Why should I be the first to dim my
headlights?' "

11

A WASP IS A GUY WHO

talks like William F. Buckley
looks like John Houseman
has the politics of Ronald Reagan
the humor of Adolf Hitler
the sure-footedness of Gerald Ford
and the fashion sense of a blind, Polish
    racetrack tout.

The airport was fogged in, so Swanton had to get home by rail. He staggered off the train. "Riding backwards for six hours," he explained, "was a perfectly horrid experience."

"Why," asked his wife, "didn't you ask the person sitting opposite to change seats with you?"

"I couldn't do that," said Swanton. "There wasn't anybody there."

*　　*　　*

Blalock walked into a store to buy a brassiere for his wife. "What size?" asked the salesgirl.

"I'm not sure," answered the husband.

"All right," said the clerk. "Is she a grapefruit?"

"No," he said.

"Is she an orange?"

"No!"

"Perhaps she's an egg."

"That's it!" said Blalock. "An egg—fried."

*　　*　　*

OSTERVILLE OPTIMIST

A WASP who thinks his wife has quit smoking cigarettes when he finds cigar butts in the house.

*   *   *

Henley had been shipwrecked on a desert island for ten years. One day a beautiful naked woman was washed ashore on a beer barrel.

Henley revived her. "Now that you've been so good to me," she said, "I'm going to give you something you haven't had for ten years."

"You mean," he exclaimed, "there's some beer in that barrel?"

*   *   *

"How did you get so banged up?" the doctor asked his patient as he applied the iodine.

"It was all a mistake, Doctor," replied Rutherford. "I came home drunk last night. And while I was making love to my wife, I got so carried away, I said, 'Honey, you're almost as bad as my wife.' "

*   *   *

Did you hear about the WASP who returned from lunch and saw a sign on his door, BACK IN 30 MINUTES, so he sat down to wait for himself?

*   *   *

Creedmoor, a midwest art dealer in New York on a business trip, took an evening off to visit one of the town's houses of pleasure. Creedmoor handed the madam a hundred-dollar bill and asked for the homeliest girl in the place. The madam was perplexed.

"Why would you pay a hundred dollars for the homeliest girl in the place?"

"I'm homesick," he said.

* * *

Paddington, about to be a father, nervously paced up and down the hospital corridors. Finally, the nurse stopped him.

"Congratulations," she said. "You have twins."

"Wonderful," said the new Daddy, "but please don't tell my wife—I want to surprise her."

* * *

The squeaking of the bedsprings increased in intensity. Then, silence. Polly's quiet voice broke the stillness of the darkened room.

"I'm not myself tonight," she insisted.

"Well, whoever you are," he sighed, "it certainly is an improvement."

* * *

Clive Baldwin, the terrifically talented Jolson sound-alike, loves telling this tall tale:

A great big Texan walked into church to pray. A poor Mexican knelt beside him and began praying loudly. The Texan shouted, "Lord, Ah want you t' see to it that mah 23rd oil well comes in real soon. That mah pork belly futures go up 50 points, and that mah brother and me completely corner the silver market."

The Mexican started to cry, "Please God, give me food for my family, a place to sleep, a job!"

The Texan said, "Will yew stop yer belly-achin'! Ah'm tryin' ta talk big business here!"

17

Mummy: I had to marry you to find out how stupid you are.

Daddy: You should have known that the minute I asked you.

*   *   *

Their marriage had ended up in the divorce court, deluged with hard feelings. Now, a year later, they happened to meet at a Sunday brunch. After both had had a few Bloodies, he put his arm around her shoulder. "Bambi," he said, "for old time's sake, let's go to bed!"

"Over my dead body!" she snapped.

"Nothing has changed, has it?" he sneered.

*   *   *

Shackleford had sued his wife for divorce and named his best friend, Trip, as corespondent.

"When did you first suspect?" asked his lawyer.

"Trip and my wife had this passion for horses. They used to go riding in the park. Then one day I noticed when they came back, they were winded and the horses weren't."

*   *   *

The motorcycle cop frantically waved the Middleburg motorist over to the curb. "Your wife," said the policeman, "fell out of your car at the last turn."

"Thank goodness," replied the motorist. "I thought I'd suddenly gone stone deaf."

*   *   *

The Canfields were riding on a train for the first time. They brought bananas for lunch. Just as the husband bit into his banana, the train entered a tunnel. "Did you take a bite of your banana?" he asked his wife.

"No."

"Well, don't!" replied Canfield. "I did, and went blind!"

*   *   *

Old-fashioned Wylie approached Sandi's Daddy, intent upon asking him for her hand in marriage.

"Sir," he blurted out, "I have an attachment for your daughter, and—"

"See here, young man," interrupted her Daddy, "when my daughter needs accessories, I'll buy them myself."

*   *   *

Mummy: Would you sooner lose your life or your money?

Daddy: My life, of course. I'll need my money to have the tennis court resurfaced.

* * *

Fenston and his wife went to the State Fair. He was fascinated by the open cockpit airplane rides, but Fenston balked at the $25 tickets.

"Tell you what," said the pilot. "If you and your wife can take all my loop the loops without making a single sound, I won't charge you anything. Otherwise you pay the $50."

"You got yourself a deal," said Fenston.

So up they went. When they got back, the pilot said, "If I hadn't been there, I never would have believed it. You never made a sound!"

"It wasn't easy, either," said the WASP. "I almost yelled when my wife fell out!"

* * *

"Daddy, why do you write so slow?" asked Loren.

"I have to," replied his father. "I'm a slow reader."

* * *

Lindsay took his son to see a show that featured fifty of the most daringly undressed girls in the country. "Phooey, phooey, phooey," Lindsay kept muttering.

"Whatsa matter, Dad? Don't you like the show?"

"Sure I do," he replied. "I was just thinking of your mother."

*   *   *

"The batter stuck to my pan," the Prides Crossing wife sobbed.

"I thought you looked better today," replied the husband.

*   *   *

"I got a A in spelling," Byron told his Dad.

"You dope!" he replied. "There isn't any A in spelling."

*   *   *

"Daddy," said Hubert, "I read in school that animals have a new fur coat every winter."

"Be quiet!" said his father. "Your mother's in the next room!"

*   *   *

Harry Rhinehart, the Pennsylvania philanthropist, fractures friends with this funny:

Podewell was discovered by his wife one night standing over their baby's crib. Silently she watched him. As he stood looking down at the sleeping infant, she saw in his face a mixture of emotions: disbelief, doubt, delight, amazement.

Touched by his unusual display and the deep emotions it aroused, Mrs. Podewell took her husband's hand.

"A penny for your thoughts," she said.

"It's amazing!" he replied. "I just *cahn't* see how anybody can make a crib like this for just $99.98."

"What a boy you are for asking questions," said Danforth. "I'd like to know what would have happened if I'd asked as many questions when I was a boy."

"Perhaps," said his son, "you'd have been able to answer some of mine."

At dinner, Tip said to his father, "Dad, I got into trouble at school today and it's all your fault."

"How's that?" asked the master of his Topsfield house.

"Remember I asked you how much $500,000 was?"

"Yes, I remember."

"Well, 'a helluva lot' ain't the right answer."

Dean: I hate to tell you this, Mr. Mead, but your son is a moron.

Mead: What! Where is that young good-for-nothing? I'll teach him to join a fraternity without consulting me!

"Son, when you grow up I want you to be a gentleman."

"I don't want to be a gentleman, Dad, I wanna be like you."

* * *

Reece, reading facts and figures from an insurance article in *The Wall Street Journal*, said, "Do you know, Dad, that every time I breathe, a man dies?"

"Why don't you use a little mouthwash now and then?"

* * *

"Dad," said Wink, "what is electricity?"

"Well," replied his Daddy, "I don't know much about electricity."

A few minutes later the boy said, "How does gas make the engine go?"

"Son," answered his father, "I'm afraid I don't know much about motors."

"Dad," said Wink, "what is radiotherapy?"

"Radiotherapy?" frowned his father. "I really don't know."

"Gee, Dad, I guess I'm making a nuisance of myself."

"Not at all, son. If you don't ask questions, you'll never learn anything."

* * *

Hutchinson's eyes were glued to the television set when his son tapped him on the shoulder. "Dad, will you help me find the least common denominator?"

"Haven't they found that yet? They were looking for that when I was a kid."

*   *   *

DADDY'S DILEMMA

How can I break it gently that
Next time my wife should bake,
That she should not put marbles
In her marble cake?

*   *   *

Young Barth was wheeling a baby carriage around the block in Far Hills on a very hot afternoon.

"Honey!" shouted his wife Kiki from an upper window of his house.

"Let me alone!" he called back. "We're all right."

An hour later Kiki once again pleaded, "Honey!"

"Well, what do you want?" Barth replied. "Anything wrong in the house?"

"No, deah, but you've been wheeling Tiffi's doll all afternoon. Isn't it time for the baby to have a turn?"

*   *   *

Tad looked up from the book on ancient history he was reading and asked his father, "Dad, what's a millennium?"

"Well," he muttered, "I think it's something like a centennial, only it has more legs!"

*   *   *

Bunni: Now, Whit, I want you to go around to the minister and arrange to have the baby christened.

Whit: You mean to say you're going to let somebody hit that little thing over the head with a bottle?

*   *   *

Bo and Cassie complained to the doctor that they'd been trying to have a baby for months.

"What position are you in when you ejaculate?" the physician asked the husband.

"What's ejaculation?" Bo asked.

"Well, uh, that's your climax," said the doctor.

Bo looked puzzled for a moment. Then he asked, "Do you mean the white stuff?"

The M.D. nodded.

"Well, Cassie says it's icky, so I shoot it in the sink before we start."

*   *   *

Newbold brought a backyard swing to his Southport home for his children and immediately started to assemble it. All the neighborhood kids were anxiously waiting to play on it.

After several hours of reading the directions, attempting to fit bolt A into slot B, etc., he finally gave up and called Olsen, an old handyman working in the neighboring yard.

Olsen came over, threw the directions away, and in a short while had the swing completely assembled.

"It's *beeeyond* me," said Newbold, "how you got it together without *eeeven* reading the instructions."

"Tell you the truth," replied the old-timer, "I can't read . . . and when you can't read, you got to think."

* * *

Binky and Megan were tightly locked together in bed. "You're taking an awfully long time tonight!" said Megan.

"I just can't think of anybody!" said Binky.

*　　*　　*

When Jennifer turned fifty, she went to her doctor for advice on reducing her midsection. He advised that she exercise by raising her feet over her head ten times before she got out of bed. She started the next morning while hubby Tyler, still hungover and half asleep, was in the bathroom shaving.

On the third time up, Jennifer caught her feet in the grillwork on the head of the brass bed and was stuck. She screamed for help.

Tyler stumbled into the room with his face lathered and squinted at her. "For God's sake," he mumbled, "comb your hair and put in your teeth! You look more like your mother every day!"

*　　*　　*

In a Fifth Avenue restaurant, Mrs. Beekman was overheard to tell her husband:

"Keep quiet! When I want your opinion, I'll give it to you!"

*　　*　　*

Amanda walked into the bedroom of her Alexandria home and found her husband Colby in bed with a young, long-haired beauty.

"How dare you make love to that child in our bed?" she demanded.

"She's just a poor hitchhiker I picked up on the highway," Colby explained. "She was hungry, so I brought her home and fed her. Then I saw her sandals were worn out, so I gave her that old pair you haven't worn in twelve years. Then I noticed her shirt was torn, so I gave her an old blouse you haven't looked at since 1976. And her jeans were all patched, so I gave her an old pair of slacks you never wear. Then, as she was leaving, she asked me, 'Is there anything else your wife doesn't use?'"

The Mummys

What do you call a woman who's happily married to a WASP?

Deaf, dumb, and blind.

* * *

Brinsley turned to his wife, sharing the seat with him, and said, "This train will soon go under a river."

For goodness' sake," she snapped, "don't just sit there. Close the window."

* * *

Bitsy had summoned the electrician to her Marblehead home.

Electrician: Your doorbell doesn't work, lady, because you have a short circuit in the wiring.

Bitsy: Well, for goodness' sake, lengthen it!

*　　*　　*

"Mummy, can I go outside and watch the solar eclipse?" asked Farley.

"Okay," she replied, "but don't stand too close."

*　　*　　*

"What are you reading?" demanded Prissy of her seven-year-old.

"A story about a cow jumping over the moon," replied Remington.

"Throw that book away at once," she commanded. "How often have I told you you're too young to read science fiction?"

*　　*　　*

"Here's a new book called *How to Help Your Husband Get Ahead*."

"Oh, no thank you. My husband already has one."

*　　*　　*

"I was born in Wisconsin."
"What part?"
"All of me, of course."

*   *   *

Mrs. Snidely went to a Junior League Charity Ball. She dined, danced, and drank all night long.

She left in the wee hours, and was just about to step into her Rolls when an old tramp came up to her.

"Excuse me, ma'am, could you spare some change. I haven't eaten for three days."

"I've just spent all night in there to help the likes of you," replied Mrs. Snidely. "Aren't you people ever satisfied?"

*   *   *

What did the Larchmont housewife do when she burned the meat?

She put suntan oil on it.

*   *   *

"Why does it take you so long to cook that chicken?"

"Well, the cookbook says to cook one-half hour to the pound, and I weigh 110 pounds."

*　　*　　*

Recently married Mrs. Maxwell, still wearing her apron and pearls, came rushing out of her Locust Valley house, and ran smack into her husband, who was practicing his backswing.

"Going somewhere?" he asked.

"Yes. I'm baking a cake from a recipe I heard on the radio. It said to put all the ingredients in a bowl and then beat it for five minutes. Sounds silly, but I'm on my way!"

*　　*　　*

Horton came home to find his new wife in tears. "Corki, what's the matter?" he asked.

"I wanted to fix you a nice martini," she sputtered. "I started out by rinsing off the ice cubes in hot water, and now I can't find them."

*　　*　　*

PALM BEACH PLAYLET

Beatrix:　Were you the one who saved my little boy from drowning?

Lifeguard:　Yes.

Beatrix:　(angrily) Well, where's his cap?

A WASP WOMAN

has the sex appeal of Margaret Thatcher,
dresses like Queen Elizabeth,
talks like Julia Child,
looks like Gloria Vanderbilt,
and cooks like Betty Crocker.

Rebecca Morgan, the magnificent sales motivator, evokes merriment with this winner:

Benita gave her husband Bayard a little kiss on the back of his bald head. Shocked, he dropped his newspaper. "That's the second time you've kissed me in four months, *deah*!"

"But *dahling*," she sighed, fingering her pearls, "I thought you wanted me to show a little more interest in the physical side of marriage."

* * *

How do you tell the bride at a WASP wedding?

She's the one kissing the golden retriever.

* * *

What do Haverford women think of the labor movement?

Cesareans are much less embarrassing.

* * *

Gwenny's parents were having their nightly squabble. "My Lord!" shouted Daddy, "you're so dumb you think Barnum and Bailey are married to each other!"

"What difference does it make," said Mummy, "as long as they love each other?"

* * *

Oliver watched his flat-chested wife Heather as she tried on her new brassiere.

"What did you buy that for?" he asked. "You haven't got anything to put in it."

"Listen," said Heather. "Do I complain about your wearing shorts?"

* * *

"But my *deah*," protested henpecked Horace, "I've done nothing. You've been talking for an hour and a half and I haven't said a word."

"I know," replied Winnie. "But you listen like a smart aleck."

*　　*　　*

"Chester and I are taking private lessons in French."

"But why?"

"Well, we adopted a little French baby, and we want to be able to understand him when he's old enough to talk!"

*　　*　　*

Fond Mummy: Yes, Muffin is taking French and Algebra. Say "Good morning" to Mrs. Hedgecock in Algebra, *dahling*.

*　　*　　*

Through her Larchmont lockjaw Mrs. Buxton boasted, "My son Broderick is smarter even than Abraham Lincoln. Broderick could recite the Gettysburg Address when he was ten years old. Lincoln didn't say it until he was fifty!"

*　　*　　*

OVERHEARD AT A
DARIEN COUNTRY CLUB

"My son is a kleptomaniac."
"That's wonderful! Where is his office?"

*   *   *

Mrs. Wellington stormed into the principal's office. "I'd like to know," she demanded through clenched teeth, "why my son Whitney was given a zero on his English examination."

"Now, just calm down," said the principal, "We'll get Whitney's English teacher in here. I'm sure she has some explanation."

A few minutes later, the teacher arrived.

"Why did you give my son Whitney a zero on his English final?" demanded Mummy, fingering her pearls.

"I had no other choice," said the schoolmarm. "He handed in a blank paper. There was absolutely nothing on it."

"That's no excuse," she shouted. "You could at least have given him an A for neatness."

*   *   *

Granny: How did Amory do on his history exam?

Mummy: Just *ghaaastly*! But it wasn't his fault. Why, they asked him about things that happened before he was born!

* * *

"Mrs. Huddlestone!" shouted the angry neighbor, "your son just threw a brick through our window!"

"Would you please bring me the brick?" intoned the woman, "we're keeping all the little mementoes of his childhood."

* * *

"It is amazing that Mrs. Bostwick down the street can never see any faults in her children," said Mrs. Witherspoon.

"Mothers never can," said her husband.

"What a silly thing to say! Just like a man! I'm sure I could see faults in our children, if they had any."

* * *

"Mummy," pleaded Kyle, "can I go to the zoo to see the monkeys?"

"But dahling," said Mummy. "Why do you want to go see the monkeys when your Aunt Caroline is here?"

* * *

Gillian's Mummy opened the door of their Bala-Cynwyd home and smiled at her daughter's escort. Then in her best Main Line malocclusion, she said, "Gillian was terribly sorry to break your date. But the truth is, she wasn't feeling very well, so she decided to go out with a young doctor, instead."

* * *

Boyd and Candice were chatting over cocktails. "Don't you think our son gets all his brains from me?" asked Boyd.

"Probably," replied Candice. "I still have all mine."

* * *

Did you hear about the Manchester Mummy who used to keep the baby in a high crib so that she could hear him if he fell out?

* * *

Little Kip: Mummy, can we go to a movie?
Mummy: If it isn't a gangster movie.
Kip: It's not. It's "The Two-headed Aliens Meet the Four-legged Dwarf Zombies."
Mummy: All right, dear. Just so it isn't about gangsters.

*   *   *

Mummy: I've lost quite a lot of weight.
Daddy: I don't see it.
Mummy: Sure you don't. I've lost it.

*   *   *

"Dahling," said Hillary, "I really managed to save something this month! I put a thousand dollars in the bank."

"Wonderful!" replied Icky. "It wasn't so hard, was it?"

"It was easy," she replied. "I just tore up the bills."

*   *   *

"Hello, is this the fire department?"

"Yes, lady, can we help you?"

"Please tell me where the nearest fire box is. I want to report a fire!"

*   *   *

How can you tell when a WASP bride is ugly?

Everyone lines up to kiss the caterer.

*   *   *

"Can you read Chinese?"

"Only when it is printed in English."

*   *   *

Buford arrived home in Ardmore one evening and found Chip, his three-year-old son, lighting up a cigar. He raced into the kitchen, where his wife Cuffy was preparing dinner.

"See here," Buford announced, "this is terrible. I just caught Chip lighting a cigar!"

'I'll put a stop to it right now," cried Cuffy. "That child is altogether too young to be playing with matches!"

Bunny had been brooding all day and Cob couldn't stand it. "What's wrong, sweetheart?" he asked.

"That *ter-r-rible* Dulcy Davenport next door has a dress exactly like mine," she replied, dabbing away an angry tear.

"And I suppose you want me to buy you a new one?"

"Well," said Bunny, "it's a lot cheaper than moving."

*   *   *

Channing arrived at his Hamilton home and said to his wife Pookie, "Where's yesterday's newspaper?"

"The maid wrapped the garbage in it," she replied.

"Oh, I wanted to see it."

"There wasn't much to see—just some orange peels and coffee grounds."

*   *   *

"Where did you get that new hat?" asked Mason.

"Don't worry, *deah*," said Topsy, fingering her pearls. "It didn't cost a thing. It was marked down from $90 to $45. So, I bought it with the $45 I saved!"

*   *   *

Bancroft, the big-game hunter, took his wife Leslie on her first safari.

After several weeks, they returned. The sportsman had bagged a few minor trophies, but the great prize was the head of a huge lion, killed by Leslie.

"What did she hit it with?" asked a friend, "That .303 Magnum rifle you bought her?"

"No," answered Bankcroft, "with the 1978 station wagon we rented."

* * *

"Wow," whispered Jacqueline to husband Palmer, as they entered the theater, "look who they've got tonight. My favorite actor—Nosmo King." She pointed to an electric sign.

"Dahling," said Palmer, "that sign says No Smoking."

* * *

ON A GREENWICH STREET

Traffic Cop: Now tell me, just what could the other driver have done to avoid this accident?

Woman Driver: He could have gone down another street!

* * *

Bootsie had recently learned to drive. Her husband Avery returned to their Fair Haven home one evening and was dismayed to see the car in the living room.

"How in the world did you land our car in here?" he asked.

"Nothing to it," she replied. "When I got to the kitchen, I simply made a left turn."

*   *   *

Mrs. Bromwell's car wouldn't start, so she reluctantly climbed on a bus. "Driver," she snapped, "where do I have to transfer?"

"Where are you going?"

"That's none of your business."

*   *   *

"Why are you so upset?" asked Alastair.

"The garage charged me $75 for towing my car a mile," said Daffi. "I got my money's worth, though. I kept my brakes on!"

*   *   *

"Honey, there's water in the carburetor."

"Where is the car?"

"In the lake."

*   *   *

Carlson and Gibbs were sipping happy hour martinis at the Plaza. "Did you see that in the *Times* today," asked Carlson, "we're going to send three million dollars worth of contraceptives to India?"

"You're kidding!" exclaimed Gibbs. "Couldn't they just do what my wife does—pretend she's sleeping?"

*   *   *

Did you hear about the Westchester County man who had such a loud orgasm he almost woke his wife?

* * *

THREE POINTS OF VIEW

Prostitute: Aren't you through yet?
Sex Maniac: Don't stop now!
WASP Wife: Barlow, I think the ceiling needs painting.

* * *

Delwyn arrived at his Cherry Hills home and was greeted by a sobbing spouse. *"Dahling,"* cried Brooke, "you know that cake you asked me to bake for you? Well, the dog ate it."

"That's okay, *deah*. Don't cry," said Delwyn. "I'll buy you another dog!"

* * *

Talbot carried the following excuse to his teacher one morning:

Please excuse Talbot for being absent. He had a new baby brother. It was not his fault.

* * *

Mrs. Puce complained to the telephone operator that she had been cut off while talking to her son at the Gilman School.

"Did he call you, ma'am?" asked the operator.

"Oh, no," replied Mrs. Puce. "He always calls me 'Mummy'!"

*   *   *

Caller: There's a fire in my house.
Fireman: How do we get to your house?
Caller: Don't you still have that big, red truck?

*   *   *

Newlywed Brinley arrived at his Lloyd Harbor home and found his wife Snookie sobbing convulsively. "I feel *ter-r-rble*," she told him, clenching her jaw. "I was pressing your suit and I burned a big hole right in the seat of your trousers."

"Forget it," consoled Brinley. "Remember that I've got an extra pair of pants for that suit."

"Yes, and it's lucky you have," said Snookie, drying her eyes. "I used them to patch the hole."

*   *   *

"Denton, go out and water the garden."
"But Winnie, it's raining out!"
"Well, put on your raincoat!"

*   *   *

Mrs. Calvert was reading *The New York Times*. "Here's something," she announced to her husband. " 'Scientists claim that the average person speaks 10,000 words a day.' "

"Yes, *deah*, but remember, you are far above average."

*   *   *

"Say! What're you doing with my wife?"

"See, I told you he'd never know what's going on!"

*   *   *

Mummy: (to little Allys) Now, *dahling*, show everybody how nicely you can recite. A little ship was on the—
Allys: Thea.
Mummy: It sailed along so pleasant—
Allys: Lee.
Mummy: It was the peaceful time of—
Allys: Night.
Mummy: And all was calm and—
Allys: Bwight.
Mummy: Wonderful! Now recite another one, *dahling*!

*   *   *

Putney was standing in the funeral home next to his wife's casket, greeting friends and relatives. Finally, his older brother, Bellamy, took him aside and said, "Listen, everybody's gossiping like crazy. Why in the hell did you choose a Y-shaped casket for Pamela?"

"Well," said Putney, "I came home and found her nude in bed. For once she wasn't bitching that she had a headache, so I took off my clothes and climbed on. It wasn't until rigor set in that I noticed she was dead, and then it was too late to get her legs together."

*　　*　　*

Buzz and Tiffie were making love when Buzz suddenly stopped and asked in a very concerned voice, "*Dahling*, am I hurting you?"

"No. Why did you ask?"

"Because you moved."

*　　*　　*

"I'm sorry, ma'am," said the conductor, "but your ticket is for Philadelphia and this train is going to Boston."

"Oh, no!" exclaimed Mrs. Van Dyne. "Does the engineer know he's going in the wrong direction?"

*　　*　　*

"Aren't you afraid the hot climate in Mexico might disagree with your wife?"

"It wouldn't dare."

*　　*　　*

What did the Hillsboro husband want to know when his wife Stephanie marched in and announced that the doctor said she couldn't make love?

How the doctor found out!

*　　*　　*

Brophy, the bartender, was bragging about a new icemaker the owner had installed that produced round ice cubes with a hole through the center.

"Ever see anything like that before?" he asked.

"Hell," growled Brewster. "I been married to one of them for twenty years?"

* * *

The Lovers

How do you tell if a WASP is sexually excited?
He has a stiff upper lip.

*   *   *

What do WASPs say when they make love?
Nothing.

*   *   *

How does a WASP know it's involved in a long-term sexual relationship?

It experiences increasing guilt and mounting disrespect for its partner.

* * *

What is WASP foreplay?
Buying cigarettes!

* * *

Blake and Missie were just married and leaving for Bermuda on their honeymoon. They were met at the pier by friends who had come down to see them off.

One fellow in the group noticed that the groom was carrying a large book under his arm. He roared with laughter when he saw the title: *What They Don't Teach You at Harvard Business School.* "What the hell do you want with a book like that on your honeymoon?" he asked.

"Hey," replied the bridegroom, "we'll be on the water for two whole days. That's a long time, and a guy's got to do something to keep from being bored."

* * *

How does a WASP know when his wife is prepared to have sex?
She comes to bed wearing only gloves.

*   *   *

What is a WASP's idea of an orgy?
Share splitting.

*   *   *

"How was your honeymoon?"
"Excellent, just excellent."
"And what does Trudi think of honey-
moons now?"
"Don't know. She's not back from hers
yet."

*   *   *

Frankel and Cline, two psychiatrists at
a Miami convention, were comparing notes.
"Anything unusual come in recently?" asked
Frankel.
"I'll say," replied Cline. "I've got a
woman patient from Shaker Heights who
hates her husband so much she closes her
eyes during lovemaking. She doesn't want
to see him enjoying himself."

*   *   *

Maggie: Tomorrow is our fiftieth wedding
anniversary. What shall we do?
Carter: Let's celibate!

*   *   *

How does a WASP propose marriage?
He asks, "How would you like to be buried with my people?"

*   *   *

At the club bar, Hugh was telling Berky about his trip to Europe on the QE II.

"I met this really *terrrific* French girl," he said, "and the only way I could flirt with her was with my English-French dictionary. I looked up the words to ask her to dinner. Then she looked up the words to ask me to dance. Afterwards, as we're walking down the passageway, she pulled me into her stateroom and began taking off my clothes."

"What happened?" asked Berky.

"Well," said Hugh, "there I was without the damn dictionary. I didn't know what to say."

*   *   *

WASP ALCOHOLIC

One who is more concerned with how sex interferes with his drinking than how his drinking interferes with sex.

*   *   *

Dryden was having lunch with several stockbrokers and they were discussing their wedding night.

"I did it five times," boasted one.

"Gee, I only made it four," stated another.

"I could only go three times," from still another.

"Gosh," spoke up Dryden, "I only did it once."

"Only once," razzed the others, "what was wrong with you?"

"Nothing," replied the WASP, "my wife wasn't used to it!"

*   *   *

Three bachelors were kidding Chappie, the married man among them. "You've been hitched five years now, Chappie. How is it you have no children?" asked one of them. Then trying to make a bad pun added, "Is your wife *unbearable*?"

"Or," said another guy, "is she *inconceivable*?"

"Maybe she's *impregnable*," joked the third man.

"No, guys, you're all wrong," lamented Chappie. "My wife is *insurmountable* and *inscrutable*!"

*   *   *

Dunston wanted to do away with his wife, Verna. Arsenic seemed the best way. "Don't poison her," advised Garrett, his old prep school roomie. "If you want to kill her, keep her up late, make love to her every night, and I guarantee you in 30 days she'll be dead!"

Dunston followed his friend's advice. He kept Verna up till three o'clock every morning and made violent love to her several times a night, knowing that she would die in just 30 days.

Exactly 25 days later, Verna was seen singing and whooping it up at a local disco. Dunston had lost 42 pounds. He was at home in a wheelchair, only a quivering shadow of a man.

A neighbor walked in the house and told him about Verna carrying on. "It's all right," said Dunston, smiling. "Let the crazy dame have a good time. She doesn't know that she's only got five more days to live!"

*   *   *

How can you tell the WASP woman at a nudist colony?

She's the one wearing the wire brassiere.

*   *   *

Barly and Dru had gone together for some time. He had tried time after time to make love to her, but to no avail. "I don't like it!" she said.

One day, they were window shopping and Dru saw a pair of red Pappagallo Blossoms. "Oh," she said, "I'd do anything for a pair of those pretty red shoes."

"You mean," said Barly, "that if I buy those shoes for you, you'd let me . . ."

"Yes," said Dru.

Barly bought the shoes. They drove out in the country, parked the car, and began making love. Dru twisted and wiggled with her legs high in the air.

"It's wonderful," exclaimed Barly, "but I thought you didn't like it."

"I don't. I'm only trying on my pretty red shoes."

*   *   *

Chilt and Cuffy were having Bloodies at the Wise Fool's Pub.

"If you don't marry me," said Chilt, "I'll blow my brains out."

"Oh, would you?" said Cuffy. "It would be such a great joke on Daddy. He doesn't think you have any."

*   *   *

What is a successful WASP romance?

It's a matter of timing. The girl has to give in just before the guy gives up.

*   *   *

Holt and Barnes were sitting in the Polo Lounge.

"Say," said Holt, noticing a pretty blonde seated at a table near the window, "isn't that Hortense?"

"I don't know," shrugged Barnes. "She looks relaxed to me."

* * *

The cocktail waitress gave Pierce a long, lingering wet kiss, waved good night, and shut her apartment door. But the young stockbroker was aroused to such fervor, he broke down the door, grabbed the girl, threw her to the floor and began pumping away.

In six minutes it was all over. "You really enjoyed that, didn't you?" bragged Pierce. "I could tell 'cause your toes are all curled up!"

"Of course they're curled!" said the girl. "I've still got my panty hose on!"

* * *

Tiff: How dare you kiss me like that?
Wade: Sorry, it was just a slip of the tongue.

* * *

During a lull in the doings at the Greenville Bar & Grill, Holly impulsively said in Locust Valley lockjaw, "Let's get married, Bowie. I don't want to wait around until I'm thirty-five and have wrinkles, bags under my eyes, and a pot belly."

"Well," replied the Texas WASP, "if that's the way you're going to look at thirty-five, let's forget it."

*　　*　　*

Simone, a hooker, fell in love with Burne, a WASP Bostonian. Burne returned the affection, but he would not marry her because she was so stupid. Simone begged him to educate her, and finally he brought her to his friend Walter, who was a professor at Harvard.

Walter taught the girl various subjects. After a year of intensive training, Burne tested his call-girl sweetheart and found, to his dismay, that she was just as stupid as ever.

MORAL: *You can lead a whore to Walter but you can't make her think.*

*　　*　　*

Why do so many WASP men remain single?

Tradition. Like father, like son.

*　　*　　*

"What did old Threadgill do when you told him you wanted to marry his daughter?"

"He behaved like a little lamb. He said, 'Bah. . . .' "

*　　*　　*

71

Alden and Seward were relaxing at the Kansas City Country Club bar. "I came home last night," said Alden, "and I found my wife sitting on the couch in the den making love to some other guy."

"*Rrr*eally?" said Seward. "I certainly hope you knew how to handle it!"

"I certainly did! I fixed them, all right. I turned out the light so they couldn't see what they were doing!"

*　　*　　*

Where can a WASP woman always get a date?

At the ASPCA.

*　　*　　*

How long does a WASP spend in finishing school?

As soon as she finds a man, she's finished.

*　　*　　*

"I really don't know what you see in him, my *deah*," said Amelia to her daughter. "He's just an everyday sort of man."

"Gee," was the response, "what more could a girl ask for?"

*　　*　　*

"Boy, do I have an absentminded milkman," announced Archibald to his golf partner, Shelby. "This morning, my wife Bunnie wasn't feeling too well, so I stayed home a little longer to take care of her. All of a sudden I hear the milkman at the back door. I'm not dressed, so I grabbed the nearest thing—Bunnie's bathrobe—threw it around me, and answered the knock."

"So?" asked Shelby.

"So this nut grabs me in his arms and starts hugging and kissing me!"

"So?"

"So, can you imagine the coincidence? The milkman's wife must have a bathrobe just like Bunnie's!"

* * *

Braden called Glenna at Sarah Lawrence for a date.

"But Braden, I've got my menstrual cycle!"

"So, I'll come over on my Moped!"

* * *

Van: I had a dream about you last night.
Pam: Did you?
Van: No, you wouldn't let me.

* * *

Brink picked up Steffi at the Radcliffe dorm and took her for a drive. They came to a quiet spot out in the country, and the car stopped.

"Out of gas," said Brink.

Steffi picked up her purse, opened it and pulled out a bottle.

"Wow!" exclaimed Brink. "You've got a whole pint—what kind is it?"

"Gasoline," replied Steffi.

Gigi disobeyed her Cape Cod parents and married a Greenwich Village street musician. A week later he told her, "Listen, chick, if you don't like the way things are going, you can blow."

The bride squealed, "Sweetheart, I'll do anything to make you happy, but will you please wash first?"

*   *   *

Catherine came to her Chevy Chase home very excited about Bartholomew, the new fellow she had met at Dartmouth. Upon questioning her, her parents learned that they had once known the boy's parents.

"His father was very homely, but he made a lot of money in the stock market," said her mother.

"His mother was very beautiful, but she married for money," said her father.

"Bartholomew is just perfect," raved Catherine. "He's got his mother's looks and his father's money!"

*   *   *

How do you deflower a WASP?
Buy her a western saddle.

*   *   *

What's the most important item in a WASP coed's trousseau?
Her Daddy.

*   *   *

Thatch snuggled up close to Carrie and put his arms around her. His hand immediately began searching under her sweater.

"What *are* you doing?" cried Carrie.

"I'm looking for something that stretches and snaps," said Thatch.

"Well, you might as well give up," said Carrie, "because that's not where I keep my turtles."

*   *   *

What do you call a sexy WASP honeymoon?

Mission Impossible.

*   *   *

Dodge had never really made out with the ladies. Now he stared incredulously from his upper berth at a blonde getting undressed in a lower berth on the Chicago Limited.

The woman slowly took off her wig, then removed a glass eye and her falsies. As she reached down to unscrew her wooden leg, she spotted Dodge peeping at her. "What do you want?" she asked.

"You know what I want!" slobbered Dodge. "Unscrew it and throw it up here!"

*   *   *

Constance had been married just a month, and after a big fight, returned home. "Now, Constance," said her mother, "I don't know how you can say Toby doesn't love you. Why, with my own eyes I saw him cry over your hand when you cut your finger."

"Sure," said Constance, "that was just to get salt in the wound."

*   *   *

Meredith allowed herself to be picked up at Diamond Lil's, and after a few drinks, went to the guy's apartment. While he was changing into "something more comfortable," Meredith was intrigued by a large brass button marked PUSH.

She pushed, a secret panel slid up, and she stepped into a completely outfitted torture chamber, with whips, branding irons, and pokers.

Meredith froze when she noticed that the windows were barred and the door bolted. Frightened, she ran into the den. Animal heads decorated the walls here. The Grosse Pointe beauty began to tremble.

Suddenly her host entered behind her, wearing a puce silk robe, his eyes slit evilly.

"W-w-what are you going to do to me?" she stammered.

While she cowered in fear, he looked
at her and said, "I'm going to rape you!"
"Oh, thank God!" she sighed.

*   *   *

The Clergy

"I made seven hearts very happy today," the minister told one of his parishioners.

"How's that?"

"Well, I married three couples."

"That only makes six," said the parishioner.

"Well," said the cleric, "you don't think I did it for nothing, do you?"

*   *   *

A little boy in church awakened after a nap and asked his father, "Has the preacher finished yet?"

"Yes, Benton, he has finished—but he hasn't stopped."

*   *   *

Willingham was the new minister. His first sermon lasted only fifteen minutes. His second one went on for thirty minutes. But his third sermon ran about two hours.

Willingham was called by the board to explain why the length of the sermons was so varied.

"Well," said the minister, "the first time I had just had all my teeth pulled and my mouth was sore.

"The second sermon was just after I had my new dentures fitted and I was having difficulty keeping them in.

"But the third sermon I accidentally picked up my wife's teeth by mistake."

*   *   *

Etta: My pastor is so good he can talk on any subject for an hour.

Wallis: That's nothing! My pastor can talk for an hour without a subject!

*   *   *

Four clergymen of different religious affiliations met at a convention. They were soon discussing their own secret vices.

"I'm very partial to ham sandwiches," revealed the rabbi.

"I get through a bottle of whiskey a day," said the Baptist minister.

"I have a girlfriend on the side," admitted the Catholic priest.

The rabbi turned to the Protestant minister and said, "What about you—surely you have a secret vice?"

"Yes," he said. "I like to gossip."

*　　*　　*

CHURCH BULLETIN

There will be a church picnic Wednesday afternoon.
If it rains in the afternoon, the picnic will be held in the morning.

*　　*　　*

A Methodist visited Kansas City during a large Baptist convention.

"This is remarkable!" he exclaimed. "I've never seen so many Baptists in all my life."

"Oh, that's nothing," replied another visitor. "In our state, even the warden of the penitentiary is a Baptist, as well as over half of the inmates."

*　　*　　*

At a luncheon meeting of local ministers, a watermelon spiked with vodka had been served to them by mistake. The restaurant's owner waited nervously for the cleric's reaction.

"Quick," he whispered to his waiter, "what did they say?"

"Nothing," said the waiter. "They were all too busy slipping the seeds into their pockets."

*   *   *

A Protestant convention of more than a thousand delegates met for a week in Cincinnati.

"I suppose business is good, with all these delegates here?" a regular customer asked one the storekeepers.

"No," said the businessman. "They came with the Ten Commandments in one hand, a twenty-dollar bill in the other hand, and they haven't broken either of them yet."

*   *   *

Mark Twain tells about listening to a minister's sermon. "After ten minutes, I was going to put $50 in the basket. After a half hour, I was going to give $10. After an hour, I stole $2."

*   *   *

Reverend Daniels was winding up his Sunday sermon. "Recognize what the good Lord has done for each one of you. Surely you should give at least one tenth of all you earn to the Lord."

"Amen!" shouted Farmington from a rear pew. "I say let's raise it to one twentieth."

*   *   *

One evening Rabbi Roth attended a forum presented by Population Zero advocates. The speaker, Dr. Kingsley, an unsmiling Protestant churchman, launched an attack against modern sexual mores. Dr. Kingsley directed his fire against marital intimacies and stated that we'd all be better off without sex.

After the meeting, Rabbi Roth approached the churchman.

"Sir," he began, "you stated without any equivocation that most wives actually prefer celibate husbands. Where did you get that information?"

"From an unimpeachable source," said the clergyman. "My wife told me!"

*   *   *

What is a WASP's worst religious fear?

To be caught in church with only a $20 bill.

*   *   *

"I shall omit the blessing this Sunday," said the minister. "I don't think you need it. The Lord said 'Blessed are the poor' and, judging by the size of the collection, that covers all of you."

*   *   *

"I've been racking my brains, but I can't place you," Daulton said to a man at a gathering. "And you look very much like somebody I have seen a lot—somebody I don't like, but I can't tell you why. Isn't that strange?"

"No," said the other man. "You've seen me a lot and I know why you resent me. For two years I passed the collection plate in your church."

*　　*　　*

At a county fair the "strong man" was showing his amazing strength. Taking a lemon, he squeezed it until the last drop of juice had been removed.

"I'll give a hundred bucks to anyone who can squeeze one more drop out of this lemon," he offered.

Several big, husky men tried, but failed. Boynton, a little scrawny man with glasses, then took the lemon. He grasped it in his hand, squeezed it, and juice simply poured out.

"Remarkable," exclaimed the strong man. "How'd you do it?"

"It was easy," said the little man. "See, I'm the treasurer of the First Methodist Church."

*　　*　　*

A visiting minister remarked at the beginning of his sermon that he felt right at home with them. "I saw all these empty seats up front, I felt the gum under my bench, and when I saw the size of the offerings, I knew I was among friends. You surely are my people."

*   *   *

A congregation decided to raise the minister's salary from $18,000 to $20,000, and called on him with the good news.

But the minister wouldn't hear of it, for three reasons: "First, because you can't afford to give me more than $18,000. Second, because my preaching is not worth more than $18,000. And third, because the added task of trying to collect an additional $2000 from you would probably kill me."

*   *   *

A minister told his flock that he had received a call to go to another church. One of the deacons asked him how much more he was offered. The minister answered, "Five hundred dollars."

"Well," said the deacon, "I don't blame you for going if you want to, but you should be more exact in your language, Parson. That isn't a call, that's a raise."

*   *   *

Thornton purchased a horse from Reverend Whitefield. ''I'm a very religious man,'' said the minister. ''I've owned the horse since it was a colt. It responds only to 'Amen' when you want it to stop and 'Thank Heaven' when you want it to go.''

The money was exchanged, Thornton climbed on the horse and galloped off. As the horse raced across the open plain, it headed straight for a cliff.

''Amen!'' shouted Thornton. The horse stopped just a few feet from the edge of the cliff.

The new owner mopped his brow and breathed a sigh of relief.

''Thank Heaven,'' he said.

* * *

CHURCH BULLETIN

In the future the preacher for next Sunday will be found hanging on the notice board.

* * *

Several churches in the South decided to hold union services. The leader was a Baptist and proud of his denomination.

"How many Baptists are here?" he asked on the first night of the revival.

All except Mrs. Murchison raised their hands.

"Lady, what are you?" asked the leader.

"I'm a Methodist," she replied.

"Why are you a Methodist?" queried the leader.

"Well," exclaimed the woman, "my grandparents were Methodists, my mother was a Methodist, and my late husband was a Methodist."

"Well," retorted the leader, "just supposing all your relatives had been morons, what would that have made you?"

"Oh, a Baptist, I suppose," replied the woman.

* * *

At a church meeting everyone was asked to write down their denomination.

Hickock wrote Baptist.

"I thought you were a Presbyterian," said the man next to him.

"I am, but I didn't know how to spell Presbyterian."

"Well, why didn't you just write a P?"

"I thought about it, but I was afraid everybody would think I was Piscopalian."

*　　*　　*

Bagley and Mead, two ministers of different faiths, were the best of friends, but often disagreed on religious issues. One day they had been arguing a little more than usual on some theological point when Bagley said, "That's all right. We'll just agree to disagree. The thing that counts is that we're both doing the Lord's work . . . you in your way, and I in His."

*　　*　　*

A minister visited a family where the father had just died. He asked the young son, "What were your father's last words?"

"He didn't have any," said the boy. "Mummy was with him to the end."

*　　*　　*

A Methodist minister was phoned by Mrs. Dinsworthy, who was quite ill. She asked him if he would be kind enough to come to her bedside.

When he arrived, the minister said to the woman's ten-year-old son, "I'm most happy your mother called me. Only, tell me, is your Protestant minister out of town?"

"Not at all," replied the boy. "Mummy just said she was afraid she might have a sickness that was contagious."

*   *   *

Bishop Bundy was invited to the home of a wealthy church contributor for dinner. He noticed a big dog in the corner keeping a sharp eye on him. Every time Bundy took a bite, the dog's eye followed his hand. The bishop exclaimed, "This surely is the most intelligent dog I ever saw. He seems to be interested in my every bite."

"Yes, he is. You see, you are eating out of his plate."

*   *   *

Reverend Maxwell was traveling aboard a jet for the first time and seemed a little nervous. The flight attendant asked, "Would you care for a drink?"

"No, thanks," he said. "We're too close to the head office."

Pastor Griffith wasn't getting results in his little church and was going to resign. He decided, however, to preach one more sermon and to make it his best.

That Sunday morning he illustrated a point in his sermon by pointing out that some flowers require much sunshine, while others, such as begonias, thrive in shady places.

After the service old Mrs. Ashcroft approached the pastor. "Oh, it was such a good sermon," she enthused. "I can't tell you how I appreciate it."

"Thank you," exclaimed the minister. "I was beginning to think I was not doing so well."

"Nonsense," said the woman. "I had no idea why my begonias weren't growing."

*   *   *

Did you hear about the minister who decided to brighten up Sunday school activities and make them more appealing for modern youth?

He installed a stereo, a coffee bar and a disco, booked pop groups, let the boys and girls mix freely together, allowed them to smoke, and encouraged them to talk freely about their problems. Attendance dropped to nil.

Parents claimed that Sunday school was no fit place to send their children.

* * *

Then there was the sad young WASP whose girl refused to marry him for religious reasons. He was broke, and she worshipped money.

* * *

A minister's daughter named Claire
Was having her first love affair.
    As she climbed into bed,
    She reverently said,
"I wish to be opened with prayer."

* * *

Tushingham had been rector of St. Matthews Church for many years. He was prim and proper beyond words. Everyone was shocked when he suddenly announced his marriage.

Tushingham had been away with his bride for a week, and when he returned, everyone was consumed with curiosity.

One of the choirboys thought it only civil to ask about his honeymoon.

"Tell me, Reverend," asked the boy, "how did you find it?"

Tushingham thought for a moment and then said, "With difficulty."

The lad looked at him blankly. The minister murmured to himself, "Who would ever think of looking under all that hair!"

Beazley, Hedge, and Windham went to Grand Central Station to get a train to Pittsburgh for a meeting of the Protestant hierarchy. The elder two appointed Windham to buy three tickets. Behind the counter stood a blonde wearing a low-cut dress that exposed her Dolly Parton-like charms. The young minister was visibly flustered.

"Let me have three pickets for Titsburgh," he blurted out.

Terribly embarrassed, Windham ran back to the other clergymen.

Hedge took the money and approached the window.

"Can I have three tickets for Pittsburgh?" he asked. "And I'd like my change in nipples and dimes."

He was so abashed, Hedge left the tickets on the counter and ran back to the others. Beazley, the eldest, then approached the counter.

"Miss," he said, "if you go around dressed in such a provocative manner, judgment will be passed on you at the Pearly Gates. I am bound to tell you that St. Finger will surely be there pointing his peter at you. . . ."

*   *   *

Wesley and Tennant, two missionaries in Africa, were captured by a tribe of cannibals and placed in a large pot of water suspended over a huge fire.

A few minutes later, Tennant began to laugh uncontrollably.

"What's wrong with you?" snapped Wesley. "We're being boiled alive! They're going to eat us! What could possibly be funny at a time like this?"

Tennant giggled. "I just peed in the soup!"

* * *

A bishop was speaking with some feeling about the use of cosmetics by girls.

"The more experience I have of lipstick," he declared, "the more distasteful I find it."

* * *

Why do Baptists forbid fornicating standing up?

They're afraid it just might lead to dancing.

* * *

The chairman was announcing the award of the church raffle prizes. "To begin with," he declared, "third prize belongs to Mrs. Loomis, a Mercedes. . . ."

Peabody, who had won second prize, became very excited. The chairman continued, "Second prize is this lovely cake!"

"A cake!" exclaimed Peabody. "What kind of prize is that?"

"Perhaps you don't realize," admonished the chairman, "that this cake was baked by the minister's wife."

"Who cares," shouted Peabody. "Screw the minister's wife!"

"That is Mr. Bleecher's right," replied the chairman. "He won the first prize!"

* * *

The Reverend Hedley van Smedley
Pulled on his tool very steadily.
    It grew fourteen inches
    And now in the clinches
He rams home a gadget most deadly.

* * *

A lady of leisure stopped at a little midwest town. Soon she received visits from the town's male population, young and old, married and single. Her admirers were so hot to trot that they visited her again and again.

Finally, the elders of the church met and determined to stop the young woman's operations. A committee of three called on the girl at her house.

"We must approach her gently," said the deacon, "and persuade her to leave without a scandal. You gentlemen wait here and I'll go up and talk to her."

One hour later, the deacon finally came down and reported to the others.

"There must be some mistake," he said, "this young woman has been grossly maligned. I found her to be a highly cultured piano teacher and not a prostitute. We have no right to force her to leave."

"All right, Deacon," replied one of the others, "if that's your final opinion, zip up your pants and let's go!"

* * *

The suburban minister decided he should do something about the orgies rumored to be going on at a suburban house. One night he rang the bell repeatedly until finally a man, completely naked, opened the door.

"What can I do for you, Reverend?" he asked.

"I suspect there is an orgy going on in this house," said the clergyman.

"There is," admitted the guy. "Right now all the ladies are blindfolded and are trying to guess which dick belongs to whom just by feeling it. I think you ought to come in and join the party, Reverend, because your name has come up five times."

*　　*　　*

Delbert went to a house of ill repute and asked the madam to supply him with a girl who had herpes. "I assure you none of my girls are sick," said the woman. "Why on earth do you want such a thing?"

"I want to catch it so I can give it to our housekeeper," said Delbert.

"What kind of monster are you?" exclaimed the madam. "What have you against the poor girl?"

"Nothing," explained Delbert, "but she'll give it to Daddy. He'll give it to Mummy, and she'll give it to the minister. That's the son of a bitch I'm after!"

*   *   *

CHURCH NOTICE

The regular church service will commence next Sunday at 3 p.m. and continue until further notice.

*   *   *

Ashmore died and went to heaven. St. Peter offered to show the new arrival around. As they walked from place to place, St. Peter pointed to the different groups and explained who they were.

"They're the Jews . . . those over there are Buddhists . . . these are Catholics . . . the ones in the corner are Mormons . . ."

They arrived at a compound surrounded by a high wall. From inside could be heard the sound of voices and laughter.

"Who are those?" asked the new arrival.

"Hush!" said St. Peter, "They're the Protestants, but they think they're the only ones here."

*   *   *

The Preplings

It is terribly important for WASPs to obtain official WASPhood training in prep schools. The education provided by Mary Institute, Bryn Mawr, the Episcopal Academy, and other posh preparatory institutions is of the highest caliber. The following are some history test answers turned in by the future corporation executives, financial advisors, statesmen, ambassadors, and U.S. presidents:

Seats of congressmen are vaccinated every two years.

The American government finally decided to put all the Indians in reservoirs.

The Mason-Dixie Line divides the country into Mason to the North and Dixie to the South.

The Thirteenth Amendment to the Constitution abolished the Negroes.

One of the rights people enjoy under the Constitution is the right to keep bare arms.

The Romans prosecuted the early Christians because they disapproved of gladiola fights and would not burn insects before the statue of the emperor.

During the age of chivalry the knights lived in manures and had many manurial rights.

Mercury was the god of the weather because he is found in thermometers.

Milton was a blind poet who wrote *Paradise Lost*. When his wife died, he wrote *Paradise Regained*.

King Henry III of England had a large abbess on his knee, which made walking difficult.

Hamlet is an English dish consisting of ham and eggs cooked together.

Cleopatra died when she was bitten by an ass.

A papal bull was a ferocious bull kept by the popes to trample on Protestants.

The Red Sea and the Mediterranean Sea are connected by the Sewage Canal.

The climate of Bombay is such that its natives have to live in other places.

The Black Hole of Calcutta had only one small widow, and more than a hundred Englishmen died when they were shut up there for the night.

*   *   *

Ten-year-old Thatcher, under the guidance of his grandmother, was becoming something of a Bible student.

He approached her with this question: "Granny, which virgin was the mother of Christ—the Virgin Mary or the King James Virgin?"

*   *   *

"Now, Prentice," said the teacher, "can you tell me what a hypocrite is?"

"Yes, ma'am," replied Prentice. "It's a boy who comes to school with a smile on his face."

*   *   *

Each year a private school presented a classical play like *Hamlet, Macbeth,* or *Romeo and Juliet.*

A few days before the annual performance was to take place, the fifth-grade teacher decided to prepare her class for it.

"Does anyone know who Shakespeare is?" she asked.

Barclay raised his hand. "Sure," he answered, "he's the guy who writes the eighth-grade plays every year."

*   *   *

What do Attila the Hun, Alexander the Great, and Smokey the Bear have in common?
They all have the same middle name.

*　　*　　*

New Neighbor: Hello, little boy. What's your name?

Little Boy: My name is Cornelius. Are you the "Awful People" who just moved next door?

*　　*　　*

A history instructor in the Dalton School asked one of her pupils, "Who was Magellan?"

The boy answered, "He's the guy who circumcised the globe."

*　　*　　*

BOYS' ROOM GRAFFITI

I don't like the teacher,
The subject's too deep;
I'd cut the class
But I need the sleep.

*　　*　　*

Berkie: Sir, can I be punished for what I haven't done?

Master: Of course not.

Berkie: I haven't done my homework, sir.

*　　*　　*

Young Brandon and his parents were at the train-station bar when they heard a whistle. Mummy and Daddy gulped down their Bloodies and the three of them rushed out onto the platform, only to discover that they missed the train.

"Next one's in one hour," said the stationmaster.

The three went back into the bar. Mummy and Daddy had martinis, Brandon had a Coke.

Again they heard a whistle, rushed out, and discovered the train pulling away.

"Next one is sixty minutes from now!" said the stationmaster.

An hour later, Brandon, with Mummy and Daddy, raced out onto the platform, and his parents leaped onto the train as it pulled away. The boy was left standing on the platform, and began to laugh uproariously.

"Your parents just left you," said the stationmaster. "Why are you laughing?"

"They came down to see me off!"

*　*　*

What are the two most memorable days at prep school for a WASP?

The day he's accepted. And the day he's kicked out.

*　*　*

After his first year at St. Mark's School of Texas, Holister returned to the ranch and announced that he was a whiz in arithmetic.

"What's one and one?" asked his father.

"We haven't gotten that far yet," said the boy.

*　*　*

On the phone from prep school. "Daddy, I'm supposed to tell you that there will be a small parent-teachers meeting tomorrow night," said Kilby.

"Well, if it's going to be small, do I have to come up?" asked the father.

"Oh, yes," replied the boy. "It's just you, me, the teacher, and the principal."

*　*　*

"Dear Dad: Let me hear from you more often, even if it's only five or ten."

*　*　*

Lanceford had been finding it rather expensive to keep his popular son in the St. Louis Country Day School. One evening he returned to his Gates Mills home and was met at the door by his wife.

"I can't wait to tell you, dear!" she cried. "You know those economy lessons you've been giving Geoffrey? Well, they're finally beginning to bear fruit. He told me today what he wants for his birthday, and it will only cost 95¢!"

"Oh?" beamed Lanceford. "What does he want?"

"Just one little thing," said the wife. "He wants his own set of keys to the car!"

* * *

Skip: Did you make the debating team?
Trip: N-n-n-no, they s-s-s-said I wasn't t-t-t-tall enough.

* * *

The teacher at a posh New England prep school was trying to instill perfect honesty in her students. She insisted they write a pledge that they had not received help during the examination when they'd finished. Claudia handed her paper in. The teacher flipped to the back of the test and read, "I haven't received any help in this examination. God knows I couldn't have given any."

*   *   *

Remember, you can put a teenage Prepling in jail, but you can't stop his face from breaking out.

*   *   *

"Today's examination," said the prep school instructor, "will be conducted on the honor system. I want everybody to take seats three desks apart and in alternate rows."

*   *   *

Joan Minninger, the marvelous memory expert, reminds friends of this delightful mirthmaker:

At the age of two, Worthington wandered from his Chestnut Hill home and was lost in the forest. A pack of wild dogs found the boy and raised him until he was discovered by hunters at the age of fourteen.

*   *   *

After her weekly voice lesson, Crissy asked the teacher, "Do you think I will ever be able to do anything with my voice?"

"Well," said the instructor, "it might come in handy in case of fire or shipwreck."

*   *   *

Blane: You must marry me. I love you.
There can be no other.

Corkie: But I don't love you. You must find some other woman, some beautiful woman.

Blane: But I don't want a beautiful woman. I want you!

* * *

How can you tell a WASP teenager?
He's the kid whose alligator has acne.

* * *

A romantic St. Lawrence Prepling embraced her boyfriend passionately. "Isn't it wonderful?" she cooed in his ear. "We're just like Romeo and Juliet. Daddy says he's going to kill you!"

* * *

They met at a Hawken School dance.

"You're really a very pretty girl," said Chilton.

"Now, now!" said Jinny. "You'd say so even if you didn't think so!"

"Sure. And you'd think so even if I didn't say so."

* * *

The youngster had an incredibly high I.Q. In three years he made it through the Lovett School and Phillips Academy.

Two years later Worthington graduated from MIT summa cum laude in nuclear physics.

He was destined for an extremely brilliant future—but he was killed one day trying to bite the tires on a speeding car.

Clerk: This is a lovely valentine . . . such a stirring sentiment: "To the only boy I ever loved."

Emmie: That's fine. Give me a dozen, please!

*   *   *

Melinda was a senior at the Foxcroft School and had been dating Cameron for some time. They were horseback riding when Cameron blurted, "I've lost all my money. Even my inheritance. I haven't a cent in the world."

"That won't make any difference, *deah*," said Melinda. "I'll love you just as much . . . even if I never see you again."

*   *   *

Aboard a coastbound plane that made several intermediate stops, little Dulcie asked her Mummy, "What was the name of the city before last that we landed in?"

Mummy, engrossed in an L.L. Bean catalogue, grumbled, "How do I know? And why do you suddenly want to know, anyhow?"

"Well, for one thing," observed Dulcie, "Daddy got off there."

*   *   *

Laurel Barnard, the beautiful Bantam

School Sales exec, beams broadly over this bauble:

Little Chrissy was Mummy's helper. She helped set the table when company was due for dinner. Presently everything was on, the guest came in, and everyone sat down. Then Mummy noticed something was missing.

"Chrissy," she said, "you didn't put a knife and fork at Mr. Burnham's place."

"I didn't think he'd need them," explained Chrissy. "Daddy said he always eats like a horse."

* * *

Little Barnaby: I've got a stomachache.
Aunt Priscilla: That's because you haven't eaten and your stomach is empty, so it hurts.
Little Barnaby: I guess that's why Uncle Colbert has headaches all the time. His head must be empty too.

* * *

Little Thorpe telephoned Daddy at his office. "Hello, who's this?"

Daddy recognized his son's voice and answered, "The smartest man in the world."

"Pardon me," said the boy. "I've got the wrong number."

*   *   *

Grant: I wish I had enough money to buy an elephant.
Boyce: What would you do with an elephant?
Grant: Who cares about the elephant? I just wish I had the money.

*   *   *

A Jamestown gardener overheard his employer's child saying this nursery rhyme:
"The butcher, the baker, the Mercedes maker . . ."

*   *   *

Two boys on a Barrington street:
"Do you say a prayer before you eat?"
"No, we don't have to. Mummy just defrosts it in the microwave."

*   *   *

Mummy and Daddy were having an argument. "If you were a good father, you would take Melville to the zoo."
"I will not. If the zoo wants him, let them come and get him."

*   *   *

Meggi arrived home from a Sunday brunch and was greeted by her ten-year-old daughter. "Borden swallowed a cricket."

"Oh, my! Did you call the doctor?"

"I didn't need to. I gave him some insect powder."

* * *

"Now, Rodney, were you nice to your sister while I was at the club?"

"Yes, Mummy. I gave her half my peanuts."

"That's nice."

"I gave her the shells."

* * *

FATHER'S FRIGHT

Nothing gives a WASP
More of a chill,
Than to have his Preplings ask
If he's made out his will.

* * *

Colin: We have a new baby at our house.
Stacy: Is it a girl or boy?
Colin: I don't know, they haven't put its clothes on yet.

* * *

Barbara Foster, the keen-witted Keynote Speakers bureau prexey, loves this cutie:

Mummy was teaching young Royce to say his prayers. "You mean," he questioned, "if I pray, I'll get everything I want?"

"Eh," she hedged, "everything that is, eh, good for you, *dahling*!"

"Then why should I bother? I get that anyway."

* * *

Little Pammy insisted that she be allowed to say her prayers without any help, and her parents proudly agreed.

Wide-eyed, they heard her intone:
"Our father who are in Heaven,
Howard be thy name;
Give us this day our jelly bread;
Lead us not into Penn Station,
And deliver us from people—amen!"

* * *

During a blistering hot day, Brent and Barbara were entertaining guests for dinner. When all were seated, Brent turned to his six-year-old son, Bowen, and asked him to say the blessing.

"But Daddy, I don't know what to say," he protested.

"Oh, just say what you've heard me say," the mother chimed in.

Obediently, Bowen bowed his little head and said, "Oh, Lord, why did I invite these people here on a hot day like this!"

* * *

The Preppies

What do Dartmouth Preps consider a balanced diet?
A beer in each hand.

*   *   *

What do you call an attractive Hollins College Preppie?
A contradiction in terms.

*   *   *

How can you tell what a University of Virginia Prep has had for dinner?

Look at his shirt.

*   *   *

"Dad, I got thrown out of my college because I pissed in the pool outside my dorm."

"Come on, lots of students do that!"

"From the 14th floor?"

*   *   *

Putterford: But I don't think I deserve a zero on this paper!

Professor: Neither do I, but it's the lowest I can give you.

*   *   *

What are the two biggest regrets in the life of a Colorado College Prep?

That he has to wake up to eat and he has to stop eating to sleep.

*   *   *

How is a Preppie's rear end like a chariot?

They both swing low.

*   *   *

*   *   *

How many Preppies are registered Democrats?

You've got to be kidding!

*   *   *

Dink: Was it crowded at the party last night?
Dork: Not under my table.

*   *   *

The Dean of Women at Connecticut College ended her passionate morals and anti-sex lecture to the incoming freshmen:

"And so, girls, wherever you go, remember—you represent Connecticut. No smoking in the streets, no shorts in the classroom, no unseemly conversation on the stairs. And above all, ask yourselves, when the men bother you, 'Is an hour of pleasure worth a lifetime of disgrace?' Now, are there any questions?"

"Yes," asked a blonde in the back row. "How do you make it last an hour?"

*   *   *

What's the leading cause of spontaneous combustion at Princeton?

Fat Preps walking around in corduroy slacks.

*   *   *

Why doesn't the Goodyear blimp fly over the Sweet Briar College campus?
The women can't stand the competition.

*   *   *

A young Preppie went to Samoa
And determined that no one should know her.
One young fellow tried,
But she wriggled aside,
And spilled all the spermatozoa.

*   *   *

PREPPIE PASSION

Blessed are the pure—
For they shall inhibit the earth!

*   *   *

What can most Mt. Holyoke secretaries do at 30 words per minute?
Read.

*   *   *

Where is the only place a Pine Manor College Preppie is guaranteed to get a date?
On her tombstone.

*   *   *

129

Colin decided to quit Penn and strike out on his own. He confided in his closest friend, Rob.

"This is my locker key," he said, handing it over. "Inside is a manila envelope with all my cash, the keys to my Mazarati, my black book of nymphos and the phone number of my coke connection. If I'm not back one year from today, open the locker and take what you want."

The two friends hugged each other and Colin walked out the door.

Five minutes later Rob raced across the campus to catch Colin.

"I'm glad I caught up with you," he gasped. "You gave me the wrong key."

* * *

Did you hear about the Preppie who thought that the G spot was the place on her polo shirt where the gator was sewn?

* * *

Why are so many obscene phone calls made to Sarah Lawrence College?
The Preppies there accept them collect.

* * *

A Maryland soph I'm not namin'
Asked a Preppie he thought he was tamin',
  "Have you your maidenhead?"
  "Don't be foolish," she said,
"But I still have the box that it came in."

* * *

Mr. Howell, the English teacher, emphasized over and over again the importance of developing an extensive vocabulary.
"You have my assurance," he told the class, "that if you repeat a word eight or ten times, it will be yours for life."
In the rear row Flopsy sighed and muttered to herself, "Biff, Biff, Biff."

* * *

What do you call a Preppie scholarship?
Daddy's checkbook.

*   *   *

How many Preppies does it take to screw in a light bulb?

Four. One to call Daddy and three to run out for Diet Pepsis.

*   *   *

The Theology professor addressed his question to the attractive freshman from Grosse Pointe. "Who was the first man?"

"If it's all the same to you, sir," she replied, "I'd rather not tell."

*   *   *

"Can you give me a good example of how heat expands things and cold contracts them?" asked the teacher.

Bedford Hills' brightest student replied, "Well, the days are much longer in the summer."

*   *   *

Nothing irks a hard-pressed Preppie more than shaking out an envelope from home and finding nothing in it but news and love.

*   *   *

"In which of his battles was King Alexander the XIV of Smogaria slain?" the teacher asked her class.

"I'm pretty sure it was the last one," Philo shouted from the back.

*   *   *

Corky was explaining to his Columbia counselor why he'd never been late to school since his father bought him a car. "Of course," said the counselor, "it's faster than riding a bike."

"That's not it," said the boy. "If you don't get to school early, you can't find a parking space."

*   *   *

Professor: We borrowed our numerals from the Arabs, our calendar from the Romans, and our banking from the Italians. Can anyone think of other examples?

Creighton: Our lawn mower from the Babcocks and our ladder from the Loftons.

*   *   *

Preppie boys prefer ties with dots, suits with stripes, and letters with checks.

*   *   *

Dear Dad:

Thing$ are really $well here at $chool, but they could be better. I need $ome thing$ mo$t de$perately. I $u$pect that you will $urely gue$$ what I mean and $end $ome $oon.

Your loving $on,
$heffield

Dear Shef,

NOthing is new here. I kNOw that you are doing better NOw than you did in NOvember. Write aNOther letter soon. I want to get this NOte in the NOon mail, so I'll sign off NOw.

Aunt NOra sends regards.

Love,
Dad

*   *   *

PREPPIE

A human gimme pig.

*   *   *

A Pasadena Preppie named Breeze
Weighed down by BAs and Litt. Ds,
    Collapsed from the strain.
    Alas, it was plain,
She was killing herself by degrees.

*   *   *

Professor: Do you enjoy Dickens' novels?
Mopsy: Oh, yes, I do. Every time another one comes out, I go right down to the store and buy it.

*   *   *

"Let's cut philosophy today," Gully said to Adlai.

"I can't," replied Adlai. "I need the sleep."

*   *   *

"If all my friends who slept in class were placed end to end, they would be much more comfortable."

*   *   *

What do they call a bad case of acne at Colby College?

"Some color."

*   *   *

How can you tell a Babson College Preppie is fat?

She can dance cheek-to-cheek with herself.

*   *   *

A Bryn Mawr math teacher asked his students to add every column of figures at least three times before handing in their papers.

The next day after class, Bootsy eagerly hurried forward, smiling. "Sir," she said, "I've added these figures five times."

"Excellent!" he exclaimed. "I appreciate students who are so thorough."

"Yes, sir," she replied. "And here are the five answers."

*   *   *

Why do girl cheerleaders wear sexy outfits?

It makes the Preppie boys root harder!

*   *   *

Why were the three fraternity brothers all trying to impress a waitress they knew had herpes?

They were competing for her infection!

*   *   *

Professor: Were you copying his paper?
Archibald: No, sir, I was only looking to see if he had mine right.

*   *   *

Baxter: I want a nice room for me and my
wife.

Clerk: Okay, just sign the register. Anything else?

Baxter: Yeah, give me a pack of cigarettes.

Clerk: What brand?

Baxter: (turning to girl) What kind of cigarettes do you smoke, Miss?

A bunch of Brown fraternity brothers were tanking up at the pay-when-served campus hangout. When the waitress had delivered more beers, Barf paid for the round and then with a flourish put down a dime on the serving tray. "Are you kiddin'?" asked the woman. "Ten cents?"

"Yeah," answered the big tipper. "It's symbolic—a penny for each one of my masculine inches."

"Really!" said the waitress. "What's the extra five cents for?"

* * *

There was a young Preppie of Exeter,
So pretty, that men craned their necks at her.
    One went so far
    As to wave from his car
The distinguishing mark of his sex at her.

* * *

English Prof: Are you absolutely sure this is an original short story?
Talcott: Yes, sir.
Professor: Well, congratulations on an outstanding work, Mr. Hemingway.

* * *

What are the toughest three years for a WASP?

Being a college freshman.

* * *

"Milton, the poet, was blind," said the English professor, "and Pope was a little deformed fellow. Yet they both wrote enduring verse. Does anyone in the class know of other examples where physical infirmity was no handicap?"

Preston, the pride of Radnor, Pa., raised his hand. "What about Thomas Gray, Professor?" he asked.

"Well, what about him?"

"He had an allergy in a country churchyard, didn't he?"

* * *

"And who is the Speaker of the House?"

"Mummy."

* * *

"I am now a member of the debating team," Nathaniel told his roommate. "It's going to be a real battle of wits."

"How brave of you to go unarmed!" came the reply.

* * *

The six Yale fraternity men came weaving out of the Old Heidelberg and started to crowd themselves into the Volkswagen for the rollicking ride back home. Dudley, obviously the house president, took charge of the situation.

"Herky, you drive," he said. "You're too drunk to sing."

* * *

Did you hear about the Williams College Preppie who graduated Magna Cum Loaded?

* * *

What's the only way a Lake Forest College Preppie can get into a nudist colony?
By promising to keep her clothes on.

* * *

What are the typical measurements of a Trinity College Preppie?
36-26-36. And the other leg is the same.

* * *

What's the difference between a Holstein cow and an Oberlin College Preppie?
Fifteen pounds and Jacques Cohen espadrilles.

*   *   *

Hallwred, passing through his son's college town late one evening on a business trip, decided to pay his boy a surprise visit. Arriving at the lad's fraternity house, Hallwred rapped loudly on the door. After several minutes of knocking, a second-floor window opened and a sleepy voice asked, "Waddyah want?"

"Does Trevington Hallwred live here?" asked the father.

"Yeah," replied the voice. "Dump him on the front porch."

*   *   *

What would you call a Chinese Harvard student?

A Pleppie!

*   *   *

Muffy, a Radcliffe senior, had just received an engagement ring, and excitedly wore it to class the next day. To her exasperation, no one noticed it. After squirming through half the morning, she exclaimed loudly, "My goodness, it's hot in here. I think I'll take my ring off!"

*   *   *

Bunky and Chip, who grew up in Newport, R.I., were visiting the country for the first time.

Bunky noticed a little bug on his hand. He asked his friend, "What kind of bug is that?"

"Oh, that's a lady bug," replied Chip.

Bunky looked at it again, carefully, and said, "A *lady* bug? You certainly have good eyesight."

* * *

SEMI-VIRGIN PREPPIE

A girl who tried it once
and didn't like it.

* * *

There was a young Preppie named Alice
Who thought her vagina a chalice.
  One night, sleeping nude,
  She awoke feeling lewd,
And found in her chalice a phallus.

* * *

The Cornell biology professor pointed to Miss Poindexter and asked, "What part of the human anatomy enlarges to about ten times its normal size during periods of emotion or excitement?"

"I-I refuse to answer that question," she stammered, her face beet red. Miss Schwartz was asked the same question and answered correctly, "The pupil of the eye."

"Miss Poindexter," said the prof, "your refusal to answer the question leads me to three conclusions: One, you didn't study last night's assignment; two, you have a dirty mind; and three, your marriage will be a tremendous disappointment."

* * *

How can you spot the Connecticut College Preppie in the cow pasture?
She's the one without the bell.

*   *   *

When do Vassar Preppies start to look good?
Two minutes to closing.

*   *   *

Trev and Winthrop, about to graduate, were having a few brews at the campus watering hole.

"Have you changed much in four years?" asked Trev.

"When I first came to Princeton as a raw freshman," observed Winthrop, "I was terribly conceited. But it didn't take long for that to get knocked out of me. Now I'm one of the nicest fellows in the whole school!"

*   *   *

Whizzer held out a coin to his roommate and said, "If it's heads, I go to bed. If it's tails, I stay up. If it stands on edge, I study."

*   *   *

Archie, Jock, and Travis ran out of gas on the way back to the Wisconsin campus from a late party. They matched coins to see who would walk to town for gas. They agreed the loser would get the last remaining bottle of beer when he got back. Travis lost.

"Wait a second," he snapped, "how can I be sure you guys won't drink the beer while I'm gone?"

"C'mon," Jock said. "We're friends."

Three hours later Travis still hadn't returned. It was starting to get light.

"He's not coming back," said Archie. "Let's finish the beer and walk home."

"I heard that," said Travis, leaping out from behind the car, "and just for that, I'm not going."

*　　*　　*

What can an Amherst College Prep usually get in two guesses?
Which way an elevator's going.

*　　*　　*

Taffy visited the Barnard school nurse and inquired, "When should I take the Pill?"
"On every conceivable occasion," replied the nurse.

*　　*　　*

PREPPIE STRAPLESS EVENING GOWN

A bust truster

*　　*　　*

"Do you love me?"
"Would you let me if I didn't?"
"Yes."
"No."

*　　*　　*

Missy, a Smith sophomore, spent Easter vacation in New York City, where she met Clifford, a young Greenwich Village painter. Missy wound up her holiday with many fond memories.
A few months later the Preppie returned to Manhattan with Mummy and they at-

tended an exhibition of Clifford's paintings. As they approached an extremely provocative nude, Missy's mother noticed that the canvas bore an amazing resemblance to her daughter.

"Missy," she lockjawed, "that painting looks exactly like you. Don't tell me you've been posing in the nude!"

"Of course not, Mummy," said the girl. "H-he must have painted it from memory."

*   *   *

Buffy finished her junior year at Wellesley and decided to drive her BMW home to La Jolla.

While driving through the desert, she ran out of gas. An Indian gave her a ride, sitting behind him on his pony. Every few minutes as they rode, he let out a wild whooping yell that echoed across the desert. Finally, he deposited her at a gas station and went off with a last "Yah-hoo!"

"What were you doing?" asked the station owner, "to make that Injun do all that hollerin'?"

"Nothing!" said Buffy. "I just sat behind him with my arms around his sides holding onto his saddle horn."

"Miss," said the man, "Indians ride bareback!"

*   *   *

Dirk's Dad was appalled at his constant use of slang.

"Now see here," he exclaimed, "there are three words I never want to hear you use again. One is *gross*, another is *lousy*, and the third, *sucks*."

"All right, Dad," said the boy. "What are the three words?"

*   *   *

All of Them

How do WASPs know when it's raining?
Water gets in their noses.

*   *   *

What's a WASP gentleman?
A guy who steps on his cigarette so it won't burn the carpet.

*   *   *

How do WASP families travel?
They arrive on the Mayflower and depart on the Concorde.

*   *   *

WASP

A collection of old blood and
old money preserved in old clothes.

*   *   *

What's the only way a WASP can surely find true happiness?
Amnesia.

*   *   *

Why does a WASP spend so much time in the bathroom?
It's the only place where he knows what he's doing.

*   *   *

Fannell and Crane left their Beaverton homes to do some hunting.
Fannell: I'll bet you don't shoot that rabbit.
Crane: Oh, really! What makes you think I won't hit him?
Fannell: Your gun isn't loaded.
Crane: So what! The rabbit doesn't know it.

*   *   *

When is the only time a WASP has something on his mind?
When he's wearing a hat.

*   *   *

What's the leading cause of brain damage in WASPs?
The Prep School System.

*   *   *

What would a WASP politician be if he had a little more sense?
A moron.

*   *   *

What's the worst advice you can give a WASP?
"Be yourself."

*   *   *

THE WASP'S PRAYER

Let me meet a girl
who has already had too much to drink.

*   *   *

HOW TO IDENTIFY A WASP TOURIST

He'll be wearing a seersucker suit
White saddle shoes
Someone else will be carrying his suitcase
His wife will be carrying the Hasselblad camera
And he'll be asking directions to Harry's Bar.

How boring is Lake Forest, Illinois?
It's closed on weekends.

* * *

How many Vermont WASPs does it take to change a light bulb?
Four. One to screw it in, and three to bitch about the summer tourists.

* * *

What's yellow, pink, green, purple, red, and orange?
A WASP woman on her way to the country club.

* * *

On average, which is higher among WASP women, their IQs or their golf scores?
Their weight.

* * *

"I just saw the president flying by."
"How you know it was the president?"
"It said TWA on the plane. That means Top WASP Aboard."

* * *

What do WASPs think public transportation is?

The Larkspur ferry.

*　　*　　*

OVERHEARD IN ROLAND PARK

"How can you be so stupid and live so long?"

"I take good care of myself."

*　　*　　*

How can you tell if a WASP is well-bred?

He takes his shoes off before he puts his feet on the coffee table.

*　　*　　*

What happened when the WASP called the suicide hotline?

They told him it was a good idea.

*　　*　　*

Did you hear about the new WASP jigsaw puzzle?

One piece.

*　　*　　*

HOW TO IDENTIFY
A LOWER-CLASS WASP TOURIST

He'll Be wearing a fishing hat
Hawaiian shirt
Bermuda shorts
Hush Puppies with red socks
A Brownie Star flash around his neck
And he'll be asking directions to the
    nearest saloon.

Barrie Anderton, the sophisticated British master of bon mots, gets big bellies with this beaut:

Sanders and Baldwin, two Ohioans, were traveling through a small town in southern France. Sanders decided to stop at a little grocery and stock up on provisions. In a couple of minutes he came trotting back.

"Hey, Baldy," he said, "I just bought some eggs from a French lady, and I think I got gypped when she made change for me. I kept trying to explain, but she doesn't understand me. She keeps jabbering away in French. You speak French. Come on back with me and straighten it out."

"Sure," said Baldwin.

When they reached the French woman's shop, Baldwin tipped his hat and said, *"Madame. Parlez-vous français?"*

"Oui, oui," said the woman.

"Okay," said the WASP. "Then why the hell don't you give my buddy his right change?"

*　　*　　*

Did you hear about the WASP who was filling out an application for employment at a stock brokerage?

In the blank asking his *Church Preference*, he wrote: RED BRICK.

*　　*　　*

How does a WASP mistreat his wife?
He stays with her.

*　　*　　*

What's the fastest way for a WASP alcoholic to reform?
Divorce his wife.

*　　*　　*

How do WASP women get even with their husbands?
By staying married to them.

*　　*　　*

OVERHEARD AT A ROTARY CLUB

"Bryant Nimrod called me a jackass."
"Don't stand for it."
"What'll I do?"
"Make him prove it."

*　　*　　*

WAPSs MAKE THEIR MONEY THE OLD FASHIONED WAY— THEY INHERIT IT!

What is a real high-class WASP?
A man who can tell what wine goes good with an enema.

* * *

There was a WASP banker named Scott
Who took a girl out on his yacht,
    But too lazy to rape her,
    He made darts of brown paper
Which he languidly tossed at her twat.

* * *

What's a WASP wine connoisseur?
Someone who knows which Ripple goes with Cheez Whiz.

* * *

How can you tell there's a WASP in the woods?
The bears have built fires to keep him away.

* * *

How can you tell a WASP is unemployed?

He serves Kool-Aid at his tennis court.

* * *

Why do they say WASP women make love "cafeteria style"?

You have to help yourself.

* * *

Why do WASPs smile at lightning?

Because they think they're having their picture taken.

* * *

Huxley: I'll have you know, sir, that my ancestors came over on the Mayflower.

Penick: You're quite fortunate. The immigration laws are much stricter these days.

* * *

Why do WASPs swim only on their backs?

They don't like to get their Topsiders wet.

* * *

Why did God creat WASPs?
Somebody had to buy retail.

*   *   *

How do WASPs make up for their lack
of good looks?
In stupidity.

*   *   *

What's the difference between a WASP
wedding and a WASP funeral?
One less drunk.

*   *   *

Why is a WASP meal like a good man?
You can't keep it down.

*   *   *

What do you call a skinny Protestant?
A Wisp.

*   *   *

WASP WAGGERY

Money is not manure.
It should not be spread around.

*   *   *

Farnsworth came from Pepper Pike to New York City on a business trip. On 55th Street he noticed a vendor broiling meat on a pushcart spit. A large chunk of raw meat dangled from the side of the cart on a piece of rope. Another big chunk smoked and sputtered on the rotisserie which the vendor cranked by hand.

Farnsworth stared at the old man beside the pushcart. "Listen, old chap," he said, "sorry to tell you this, but there's no music coming from that thing, your organ's on fire, and somebody skinned your monkey."

WASP GOURMET DINNER

Dry Martinis
Weenie Beanies in Silver Chafing Dish
Cheez Whiz on Ritz Crackers
Cream of Mushroom Soup
Creamed Chicken on Converted Rice
Creamed Peas and Carrots
Cheap Jug Wine in a Crystal Decanter
Fruit Cocktail Jello with Cool Whip
Instant Coffee in Silver Pot

Attire: Black Tie or Tennis Togs

Why do WASPs enjoy having colds?
It's the only thing that'll stay in their heads for more than a minute.

*   *   *

Why are WASP women like foreign cars?
All their weight is in the rear.

*   *   *

Why do WASPs have blank bumper stickers on their cars?
They don't want to get involved.

*   *   *

Why don't WASPs put ads in the newspapers for their lost dogs?
Because they know that dogs don't read newspapers.

*   *   *

From what Boone are many WASPs descended?
The baboon.

*   *   *

How many letters in a WASP alphabet?
One. The pronoun I.

Why is it a good thing there wasn't a WASP at the Last Supper?
He would have asked for separate checks.

*   *   *

What's the most common method of homicide among WASPs?
Dinner.

*   *   *

What do you get when you cross a WASP and a gorilla?
An athletic scholarship to Princeton.

*   *   *

Why do they call wealthy WASPs the cream of society?
Because they've been separated from the milk of human kindness.

*   *   *

What do you get when you cross a WASP and a Puerto Rican?
Assault and battery.

*   *   *

THE SON-IN-LAW THEY WANTED

Harvard Law, Partner in Good Firm
  400 Family
Large Trust, Diversified Portfolio
Good Tennis Player, Top Country Club
Someone who could give daughter Family Jewels, a New Mercedes, and a European Honeymoon.

THE SON-IN-LAW THEY GOT

UC Berkeley Drop-out
Anti-Nuke Demonstrator
Aspiring Forest Ranger/Organic Gardener
Someone who gave daughter a Greenpeace Poster, a Hitchhiking Honeymoon in Borneo, and Herpes.

171

Tripler left his Sewickley home one morning when he saw a driverless gardener's pickup truck rolling slowly down the street. He ran to the vehicle, jumped in, and pulled on the emergency brake with a jerk.

A sweaty, old Italian approached him, and Tripler proudly exclaimed, ''I just stopped that truck from rolling away.''

''You jackass!'' said the gardener. ''I was-a pushin' it!''

*   *   *

"How is your headache?"
"Out playing bridge."

*   *   *

THE WASP CODE OF HONOR

Do Not Lie, Steal,
or Cheat Unnecessarily.

*   *   *

What do you get when you cross a WASP and a Black?
A conversation piece.

*   *   *

What do WASPs think Zimbabwe Rhodesia is?
A linebacker for the New England Patriots.

*   *   *

What do you call a WASP family reunion?
The annual stockholder's meeting.

*   *   *

How do you make a WASP cat happy?
Mate it with a cashmere sweater.

174

*　*　*

Brighton sat at the club bar gulping Bloody Marys all morning. The alcohol so loosened his tongue that he slammed his fist down on the bar and shouted:

"I'm a good American. There's only two things in this country I can't stand—race prejudice and Negroes!"

*　*　*

How many WASPs does it take to plan a trip to Israel?

Two. One to ask where, the other to ask why.

*　*　*

Inside every WASP there's a six-pack trying to get out.

*　*　*

WASP OBEDIENCE SCHOOL

A place where a perfectly fine dog
is trained to crap on the floor, eat the drapes,
drink from the toilet bowl,
and pass farts when guests are present.

*　*　*

175

How do WASP doggies bark?
They don't, they sniff.

* * *

Quark: Does your dog have a license?
Pilp: Heavens, no! I do all the driving.

* * *

Burnside and Whitley, two former college fraternity presidents at a Cleveland convention of securities execs, met by chance in the men's washroom. Burnside, the Yale graduate, washed his hands before urinating. Whitley, the New York University alumnus, washed hands after he relieved himself.

"At NYU," announced Whitley, "one learns to wash his hands after he relieves himself."

"At Yale," retorted Burnside, "one learns not to piss on his hands."

* * *

Simpson was driving the wrong way down a one-way street. He was finally stopped by a patrol car. "Do you know where you're going?" asked the officer.

"Yes," proclaimed Simpson, "and I must be late, for everyone else is coming back."

* * *

THE SEVEN DEADLY WASP SINS

1. Picking up the bar tab
2. Hiring a Jewish lawyer
3. Eating Japanese sushi
4. Voting for a Catholic
5. Farting in church
6. Enjoying sex
7. Shopping at K mart

Wasp Philosophy

A WASP BELIEVES:

that masturbation will
   a. drive you insane,
   b. make hair grow on your palms,
   c. make you go blind,
   d. prevent you from having orgasms later.

that women who masturbate excessively during adolescence can never be satisfied by a man later on in life.

*   *   *

A WASP BELIEVES:

that nuns
   a. are bald,
   b. and don't wear any underwear.

that women who ride horses are horny.

that the shy, silent type girl is a guaranteed lay and a real tiger in bed.

that one way to test a girl's virginity is to check her lipstick tube. If it's worn down at an angle, she is *not* a virgin and will do *anything*.

that you can't get pregnant if you make love standing up.

that truck drivers know the best places to eat on the road.

that all lesbians are built like truck drivers.

that men who cross their legs at the ankles are queer.

that the secret homosexual recognition code, known only to fags, is to wear something green on Thursdays.

*   *   *

WASP ATTITUDE TOWARD ETHNIC GROUPS

A WASP THINKS:

Chinese men tuck their hands up their sleeves to conceal daggers.

All Blacks tap dance, eat watermelon, and are hung like stallions.

Italian men screw when they wake up, on their lunch break, before dinner— and that's not counting the times with their wives.

Indians never shave, as they have no facial hair.

ETHNIC GROUPS VIEW OF WASPs

To a Black, a WASP is a person who thinks Guy Lombardo is hot jazz.

* * *

An Irishman thinks a WASP is responsible for the evils of near-beer, prohibition, and the potato famine.

* * *

A Mexican thinks WASPs eat only TV dinners and Fig Newtons.

* * *

An Italian thinks a WASP gets it up once a month.

* * *

A Jew believes a WASP eats a hot pastrami sandwich on white toast with mayonnaise.

* * *

An Asian doesn't think about WASPs at all.

* * *

About the Author

This is the 40th "Official" joke book by Larry Wilde. With sales of more than 9 million copies, it is the biggest-selling humor series in publishing history.

Larry Wilde has been making people laugh for over 30 years. As a stand-up comedian, he has performed in top night spots with stars such as Debbie Reynolds, Pat Boone, and Ann-Margret.

His numerous television appearances include *The Tonight Show, The Today Show, Merv Griffin,* and *The Mary Tyler Moore Show.*

Larry's two books on comedy technique, *The Great Comedians Talk About Comedy* (Citadel) and *How the Great Comedy Writers Create Laughter* (Nelson-Hall), are acknowledged as the definitive works on the subject and are used as college textbooks.

A recognized authority on comedy, Larry is also a motivational speaker. In his humorous keynote speeches for corporations, associations, and medical facilities, he advocates getting more out of life by developing a better sense of humor.

Larry Wilde is the founder of National Humor Month, celebrated across the U.S. to point up the valuable contribution laughter makes to the quality of our lives. It begins each year on April Fools Day.

He lives on the northern California coast with his wife, Maryruth.